ETHICS 7

ENVIRONMENTAL ETHICS

This booklet is copyright and may not be copied or reproduced, in whole or part, by any means, without the publisher's prior written consent.

© Copyright 2002
First published 2002

Abacus Educational Services
424 Birmingham Road
Marlbrook
Bromsgrove
Worcestershire
B61 0HL

ISBN 1898653 23 2

Other titles available in series:
1. Ethical Theory and Language
2. Moral Rules
3. Christian Ethics (in preparation)
4. Homosexuality
5. Abortion
6. Euthanasia

Also available:

Philosophy of Religion series:
1. Religious Language
2. The Problem of Evil
3. Faith and Reason
4. God and Proof
5. Revelation and Religious Experience
6. Life after Death
7. Miracles
8. Freewill and Determinism

Philosophy series:
1. Philosophy of Mind (in preparation)

Other titles on the Synoptic Gospels and the Fourth Gospel are also available.

CONTENTS

INTRODUCTION	4
ENVIRONMENTAL ETHICS; IMPORTANT, BUT FOR WHOM?	5
WHAT ARE EXAMPLES OF CONTEMPORARY ENVIRONMENTAL PROBLEMS?	7
Global warming	7
Destruction of natural habitats	9
Depletion of ozone layer	11
WHAT ARE SOME OF THE PHILOSOPHICAL PERSPECTIVES?	13
WHAT ARE SOME OF THE RELIGIOUS PERSPECTIVES?	31
WORKSHEET	40
EXAM QUESTIONS	41
FURTHER READING	43
FOOTNOTES	46

INTRODUCTION

This booklet has been written specifically to cater for the needs of A/AS students of Philosophy, Religious Studies and General Studies. However, it may equally be used as an introduction to environmental ethics by the interested lay person or by first year undergraduates.

The style of the booklet is similar to the style employed in other booklets in other series. It is structured around key questions that have developed from classroom experience. It also contains a section that deals with exam questions and should therefore be useful for both teaching and revision.

Philosophy, of which ethics is a part, can be great fun to both study and to teach. It is a subject that both staff and students can become fully engaged in. It is therefore hoped that learning about ethics will prove to be an enjoyable experience.

ENVIRONMENTAL ETHICS: IMPORTANT, BUT FOR WHOM?

There is increasingly little doubt in prosperous Western countries that environmental issues are important. Newspapers are filled with articles on the dangers posed by global warming, acid rain or the depletion of the ozone layer. The loss of ecological diversity due to the destruction of natural habitats warrants prime-time BBC documentaries. Westerners look with increasing alarm at the prospect of countries such as India and China attaining levels of car ownership and industrialisation comparable to that of Western countries because of the environmental damage that may well ensue.

Yet many in Developing Countries point out that to some extent this sudden discovery of an environmental conscience comes after Western countries have safely established their economic prosperity at the expense of the environment. Britain for example did much of its deforestation, production of greenhouse gases and depletion of natural resources during the industrial revolution (c. 1750-1900), thereby securing its economic future. They also point out that it is easy to campaign about the preservation of rainforests for example from the comfort of middle-class Britain. The issue looks very different from the perspective of a landless farmer in Brazil whose family faces starvation if he or she does not occupy part of the rainforest. Similarly, it is easy to express concern about the production of carbon dioxide by Indian coal-burning electricity plants from the comfort of Britain or the USA where electricity is taken for granted. They point to the hypocrisy involved, given the currently higher rates of consumption in the West compared to the Developing world.

Furthermore the environmental concerns of the poor in developing countries are often very different from the major concerns of those that cause headlines in the West. For example, the world's rural poor are generally more concerned with the loss of productive land through soil erosion (caused by many factors such as drought, deforestation or the lack of secure landholdings to allow for crop rotation), than they are by the risk of skin cancer to rich tourists sitting on the beach for too long under a decreasing ozone layer.

So in what follows it is important to keep in mind the issue of whose perspective one takes on environmental issues; that of the poor or the rich, of humans or of animals, of sentient beings or the whole of nature. The booklet will exam three contemporary environmental problems and then some philosophical and religious responses to them.

WHAT ARE EXAMPLES OF CONTEMPORARY ENVIRONMENTAL PROBLEMS?

▶ GLOBAL WARMING

It is estimated that in the next hundred years the world's temperature will on average increase by up to 5[i] °C. This does not sound like a huge temperature increase but on a global scale it will have very significant consequences. It is true that global and regional temperatures have fluctuated throughout the history of the earth caused by factors such as fluctuation in the levels of radiation coming from the sun or the "wobbles" in the earth's orbit that are believed to cause the earth's periodic ice ages. Consequently scientists debate how much current temperature increases are a result of changes in human behaviour, and how much they are simply a natural variation. Nevertheless the bulk of scientific opinion today maintains that recent temperature changes are unusual and related to changes in human practice. This is the view endorsed by the authoritative Intergovernmental Panel on Climate Change (IPCC)[ii].

▷ The causes of Global Warming

Recent Global Warming has probably occurred as a result of what is known as the "Greenhouse Effect". Greenhouses work by letting in radiation of the Sun, but then trapping the radiation of the sun thereby heating the greenhouse. The earth's atmosphere comprised of gases such as Carbon dioxide (CO^2), Water Vapour (H^2O), Methane (CH^4), Ozone (O^3) and Nitrous Oxide (N^2O), works in a similar way. It lets in radiation from the sun, but traps that radiation thereby heating the earth. Without this effect human life would never have developed on earth.

However it is thought that recent changes in human behaviour have vastly increased the amount of greenhouse gases (GHG's) in the atmosphere thereby increasing the amount of heat trapped and thus the temperature of the planet.

These changes include

- The increased burning of fossil fuels containing carbon (Coal, oil and gas) releasing Carbon dioxide into the atmosphere. This is mainly a result of Western industrialisation and current levels of car and plane use.
- The increased burning of forest areas either for fuel or to free up land for agriculture, thereby releasing carbon dioxide as the carbon stored in plants and trees is burned.
- The increasing numbers of agricultural livestock who as a result of their digestive processes release methane into the atmosphere. Methane is also released by methods of rice production, the staple food of much of the world's population.

The production of ozone as sunlight reacts with exhaust emissions, most notably from cars.

The effects

It is impossible to predict with certainty what the effects of global warming may be. There are many factors to be taken into account and they are by their nature unpredictable. Benefits may result from global warming in some areas, but most scientists agree that the negative effects will outweigh any positives. For example, James Meeks, science correspondent of the Guardian, points to a scientific consensus emerging that at least some of the following negative effects will be seen in either the short or longer term[iii]:

- Increased risk of flooding in Bangladesh as sea levels rise due to the melting of the ice-caps of Antartica and Greenland for example, and due to the fact that the water itself expands as it becomes warmer. The Nile delta would also be at risk along with other areas of land on the coastal margin. Significant numbers of human and animal lives would be put at risk.
- Famine in Africa: semi-arid regions in sub-Saharan Africa turn to desert, making the food situation for some of the world's poorest countries worse.
- Disease moves North: mosquito-borne diseases such as malaria,

yellow fever, and dengue fever spread into new territiories.
- A global increase in freak weather occurrences such as floods and hurricanes.
- Birds die: an estimated 24m geese, sandpipers, dunlins and stints have to find new breeding grounds or perish due to forestation of the Arctic tundra as temperatures rise. Polar bears starve: as global warming melts the Artic ice, the bears have less chance to fatten up on the seals they catch through the ice their weight plummets and their cubs starve.

Fears of the negative effects of Global warming were sufficient for more than 150 countries to sign the Climate Change convention at the earth summit in Rio in 1992. This was an agreement to limit man-made emissions of greenhouse gases to stop the atmosphere overheating. It was followed in 1997 by the Kyoto Protocol to give all developed countries legally binding targets for cuts in emissions from the 1990 levels by 2008-2012. After significant debate and adjustment many developed countries have signed up to the Protocol with the notable exception of the world's biggest emitter of greenhouse gases, America. A sceptical minority[iv] though still wonder with some justification whether the money that countries will have to spend in order to implement the Kyoto Protocol could be better spent solving the very real and immediate problems of poverty in the world today. Maybe they argue current generations are in dangers of being sacrificed for the benefit of later generations who may or may not face all the hypothetical dangers listed above.

▶A DESTRUCTION OF NATURAL HABITATS

There is growing global concern about the loss of natural habitats with the consequent loss of ecological diversity in terms of plants and animals. Habitats can suffer for a number of reasons. As we have seen global problems such as increased global warming can cause either desertification[v], or flooding of natural habitats. Changing patterns of human usage of land can have dramatic effects. Most notably the destruction of the Amazonian rainforest in Brazil caused largely by a combination of cattle ranchers destroying forest in order to have land for cattle grazing, and indigenous people seeking to eke out an existence in ever-decreasing areas of land. By 1997 more than 40 million hectares of Amazon jungle had already been destroyed, an area larger than the whole of Japan. In the last thirty years more than 25% of the forests of Central America have been cut down so that cattle can graze where the forest once stood[vi].

Global economic factors can have devastating local effects on natural habitats. For example, in Brazil and other Latin American countries it is the levels of debt owed to Western banks and governments that almost forces the Brazilian governments to permit largescale export of timbers from dwindling areas of forest in order to earn revenues from the trade with which to pay back debts. As one Brazilian Worker's Party leader put it, 'If the Amazon is the lungs of the world then debt is its pneumonia'[vii]. Much contemporary debate concerns the recent and widespread use of dams in S.E.Asian countries to provide energy for electricity supply to the escalating population. The construction of these dams requires the flooding of large areas of the natural habitat with the consequent loss of home and livelihood for many indigenous peoples, and the death of many animal and plant species.

Natural habitats thus face many challenges as illustrated by the following case study:

Case Study: The region of Mosquitia in Honduras[viii]

Mosquitia is a region of Honduras with a very distinctive range of natural habitats. It covers an area of 20,000 sq.km., about 20% of the territory of Honduras, and contains areas of coastline, swamp, savannah and humid tropical rainforest in the valleys of the principal rivers. These areas are host to many rare species of plant and animal. Several species of plant have been used to develop medicines for the treatment of diseases. Between 45,000 and 50,000 people live in the area. The majority of the people are indigenous Miskitos who live in sensitive relationship to their environment, having developed agricultural methods that suit their context. Other Miskitos living near the coast make a living by diving for shellfish.

However the natural habitat and indigenous people of Mosquitia face considerable threats of a similar nature to those faced by many similar regions throughout the Developing world in particular. Various non-indigenous groups see the area as a resource to be exploited for monetary profit. Areas of the Mosquitia have been colonised by loggers looking for precious species of timber in the rainforest, by cattle ranchers, by speculators looking for gold in the river and by poor farmers from other areas of Honduras looking for land upon which to house and provide for their families. These newcomers may benefit in the short-term, but any gains are temporary, as the land rapidly becomes degraded through overuse and ignorance of the ecological dynamics of the area. When one area has become exhausted, the colonisers move onto another tract of land as more people follow on behind them. Indigenous people are displaced, often suffering violence, but they can do little to resist because they rarely have legally recognised land rights. Plants and animals natural to the area also suffer, with some of them edging towards extinction.

The colonisers operate within a broader context of economic and political interests. The Honduran government is keen to let logging companies and cattle ranchers into the region since the resultant timber exports boost foreign currency coming into an impoverished, heavily-indebted country. With 4% of the population of Honduras owning 60% of the land, poorer farmers are almost forced to look wherever they can for land to farm.

Indigenous people making a living in Mosquitia coastline areas from shellfish sales are also suffering as the marine environment on which they depend is overexploited. Growing numbers of divers are competing for a diminishing resource base. Young shellfish are caught illegally before they reach the end of their reproductive lives thus cutting back their fish resources.

▶ **A DEPLETION OF OZONE LAYER:**

Ozone (O^3)functions in the earth's atmosphere as a protective layer preventing too much Ultra-violet (UV) radiation from reaching the earth's surface. The amount of ozone in the atmosphere however has been radically decreasing over the past few decades. Indeed it has been shown that between 1975 and 1984, during the southern hemisphere's spring season the ozone layer thinned to almost half of its former size .

The causes: The amount of ozone in the earth's atmosphere naturally fluctuates from season to season. However the rate of recent depletion suggests that it is not simply the result of such natural fluctuation, but rather human activity. Gases released as a result of farming and industry cause the depletion of ozone. In particular man-made chloroflurocarbons (CFC's) are known to reduce ozone in the atmosphere. Methane from increasing livestock farming also reduces ozone.

The effects: Some effects are immediate and evidence for them can be found in contemporary experience. For example, Ultra-violet radiation in larger quantities is known to produce skin cancers, and skin cancers today pose an increasing problem in many parts of the world. According to the United States Environmental Protection Authority it is estimated that there will be an additional 200,000 deaths from skin cancer in the US alone over the next fifty years[x]. However there may also be even more catastrophic, but less certain problems in the longterm. For example, it is thought that UV radiation is particularly dangerous for algae living in the sea. Algae perform a very important function at the bottom of the foodchain. Without them the consequences may be very severe affecting forms of life further up the foodchain.

WHAT ARE SOME OF THE PHILOSOPHICAL PERSPECTIVES?

Two of the key backgrounds to modern philosophical thinking on ethics are utilitarianism and the moral philosophy of Immanuel Kant. They also provide the background to much of the contemporary thought on environmental ethics.

▶ **UTILITARIAN PERSPECTIVES ON THE ENVIRONMENT**

At its most basic level utilitarianism is a philosophical method for determining morally right and wrong actions in terms of their utility or "usefulness". If an action is useful in producing happiness or pleasure for humans then it is a good action. If it fails to produce happiness or actually produces pain, then it is a bad action. Some utilitarian thinkers extend their considerations to the pleasure and pain of all life-forms that can experience pain and pleasure thus including animals in their considerations. In general therefore the end or result of an action can justify the action itself even if that action contravened traditional moral rules; the "end justifies the means". Utilitarianism was developed in the eighteenth century as a method for working out the right course of action that required no reference to God even though many of its earliest proponents still believed in some sort of God, but not one who should have any authority over matters of human ethics.

Beyond this very basic account though there are significant differences between philosophers who would label themselves as utilitarian thinkers. In particular three different varieties of utilitarianism have been identified:

Some utilitarians argue that each individual decision should be taken on the merits of each individual case itself with no reference to normal moral rules (an "act-utilitarian" approach). Others point out that society's normal moral rules should have more authority than the act-utilitarian gives them because they are known from experience to promote the overall happiness of society. They do not have absolute authority because there may be rare situations where they cease to promote the greatest happiness and hence have to be disobeyed, but in general they should have authority over the actions of individuals. This approach has become known as "rule-utilitarianism". Some more modern utilitarian philosophers have introduced one more classification of utilitarianism; "preference utilitarianism". This emphasises that human beings seek after a far more diverse range of goods than simply pain or pleasure, and that these goods cannot be reduced to the simple categories of pain, pleasure or happiness. For example, humans seek after the goods of friendship, intellectual achievement, artistic beauty, or sporting brilliance, and are willing to put up with significant hardships to get there. An action is good therefore if it allows humans to make progress towards fulfilling this far wider range of "preferences"[xi].

All these different streams of utilitarianism find their roots in the work of two philosophers, Jeremy Bentham (1748-1832) and John Stuart Mill (1806-1873). See also Booklet 2 Moral Rules in this series. Their ideas will briefly be examined and to how they might be linked to environmental issues. Consideration will also be given to perhaps the most well-known modern utilitarian, Peter Singer who has written exhaustively on environmental ethics.

▶ **JEREMY BENTHAM:**

The clearest exposition of Bentham's ideas can be found in his *Introduction to the Principles of Morals and Legislation* first published in 1789. Towards the beginning of this work Bentham sets out his basic idea;

> 'Nature has placed mankind under the governance of two sovereign masters, pain and pleasure. It is for them alone to point out what we ought to do, as well as to determine what we shall do. On the one hand the standard of right and wrong, on the other the chain of causes and effects, are fastened to their throne. They govern us in all we do, in all we say, in all we think…'[xii]

Bentham in other words is arguing that what humans should do morally is in principle identical to what they will do instinctively i.e. seek pleasure and avoid pain. It is only ignorance of what will actually bring them the most pleasure that causes humans to fail to take decisions that would maximise their pleasure. His 'principle of utility' simply recognises this fact and argues that actions are useful and therefore morally good if they serve to promote pleasure or happiness, and morally bad if they promote pain. Bentham emphasises that it is the 'greatest happiness of the greatest number' which should govern all decisions. An individual should not simply seek their own happiness, but rather that of the community of which they are part. Although Bentham is essentially an act-utilitarian he still believes that it is the function of governments and the legal system to ensure that *both* the interests of the individual and that of society are served by the actions of the members of that society. Bentham's basic principle therefore is 'consequentialist' i.e. an action is morally good if as a consequence of the action pleasure increases.

Significantly in relation to environmental issues Bentham included the pain and pleasure of *all* sentient beings in his calculations[xiii]. Any being whether human or animal that has a sensory capacity to register pain or pleasure should be considered when making a decision. Furthermore the sort of pleasures that a human experiences are not necessarily of any more worth or significance than the sort of pleasures which an animal might experience. It is only because the degree of pleasure or pain that a human can experience may be greater than that which animals are capable of, that their interests may outweigh those of animals.

This links to one of Bentham's most controversial ideas; that pleasure and pain should be measured in terms of their 'quantity' not their quality. As Bentham famously puts it 'quantity of pleasure being equal, pushpin is as good as poetry'. Bentham's contemporaries would have seen pushpin (a game popular in pubs at the time much as the game of pool is now) as a lesser pursuit than the more intellectual writing of poetry. However Bentham is stating that if someone gets as much pleasure from an activity like pushpin as someone does from a seemingly more dignified, scholarly pursuit, then both actions have equal moral worth for that individual, as long as the interests of others affected have also been taken into account.

Under the overall guidance of the 'principle of utility' individual decisions need to be taken. To assist an individual or a government to make the correct decisions, Bentham developed his 'hedonic or felicific' calculus. Basically this was a way of calculating the quantity of pleasure or pain that would result from a particular action so that the decision-maker would know whether it was the best action to undertake.

The Hedonic Calculus:

Seven aspects of the possible pleasure to be produced had to be taken into account:

Its *intensity* i.e. how intense the pleasure or pain would be to the sentient beings affected.

Its *duration* i.e. how long the pleasure or pain is likely to last for all those affected.

Its *certainty or uncertainty* i.e. how certain is it that the pleasure or pain will result from a particular action.

Its *propinquity or remoteness* i.e. how near either in terms of geographical distance or distance over time is the pain or pleasure to the person making the decision.

Its *fecundity* i.e. the chance that the pleasure will be followed by more pleasures, or that the pain will be followed by further pains.

Its *purity* i.e. the chance that pleasure will be followed by pain or that pain will be followed by pleasure. A "pure" pleasure is one followed only by more pleasure, and not made "impure" by becoming mixed with pain.

Its *extent* i.e. the number of persons who are affected by the pleasure or pain resulting from a particular action.

Bentham's general principle of utility coupled with his hedonic calculus could provide a good framework for thinking about the very complex issues in environmental ethics. Most people would agree that human pain and pleasure are important when making decisions on environmental issues. Fewer would agree that all sentient beings have the same right to be considered, but many would agree that the pointless suffering of animals for example is to be avoided. Most people recognise that in environmental dilemmas such as whether to build a dam thereby flooding an area of huge ecological diversity, a way of balancing different interests and claims is necessary. For example, the pain caused by uprooting the indigenous population (both human and animal) needs to be weighed against the pleasure that will be created by providing improved electricity supply for a city. Bentham's hedonic calculus or modifications of it might provide a method of balancing these different rights and interests. Similarly in taking the decision as to whether expensive steps to curb Global warming now are the right steps to take, a method which allowed decision-makers to calculate the relative amounts of pleasure and pain that will result might well be of considerable use. They might use it for example, to weigh up whether it is better to spend the money that could be spent curbing GHG's on fighting poverty now, against whether the well-being of future generations is so dependent on curbing GHG emissions now that the money must be spent immediately.

▶ JOHN STUART MILL

Mill summarises his thinking as follows in his essay entitled Utilitarianism:

> 'The creed which accepts as the foundation of morals, utility, or the greatest happiness principle, holds that actions are right in proportion as they tend to promote happiness, wrong as they tend to produce the reverse of happiness. By happiness is intended pleasure, and the absence of pain; by unhappiness, pain, and the privation of pleasure...pleasure and pain are the only things desirable as ends; and that all desirable things...are desirable either for the pleasure inherent in themselves, or as a means to the promotion of pleasure and avoidance of pain.'

> 'The utilitarian standard of what is right in conduct is not the agent's own happiness, but that of all concerned. As between his own happiness and that of others utilitarianism requires him to be as strictly impartial as a disinterested spectator.'

> '[The goal of utilitarian thinking is to secure] an existence exempt as far as possible from pain and as rich as possible in enjoyments, both in point of quality and quantity; the test of quality, and the rule

for measuring it against quantity, being the preference felt by those who in their opportunities of experience, to which must be added their habits of self-consciousness and self-observation, are best furnished with the means of comparison'[xiv].

The similarities between Bentham and Mill are clear concerning the basics of utilitarianism. The 'Greatest Happiness Principle' and the 'Principle of Utility' are very similar ideas, and Bentham indeed sometimes used the phrase 'Greatest Happiness Principle'. Some of these shared ideas have considerable implications for the environment as we saw when examining Bentham's ideas. For example, Mill's insistence that the decision-maker must treat <u>all</u> those affected by decision equally has clear implications for use of environmental resources. For example, as was discussed earlier, the continued levels of use of carbon-based fuels are almost certainly leading to Global Warming. This could have catastrophic effects for millions of people particularly in the future. Within Mill's system their interests need to be taken into account.

However there are some important differences between the utilitarian philosophies of Bentham and Mill which could have implications for environmental issues.

While Bentham is explicit in including all sentient beings that could be affected by a decision in the hedonic calculus, Mill does not explicitly state that they should be considered in moral decision-naming. Indeed in his famous essay entitled "Nature Mill", urges his readers to 'acknowledge that the ways of nature are to be conquered not obeyed: that her powers are often towards man in the position of enemies, from which he must wrest, by force or ingenuity, what he can for his own use'[xv]. However implicitly he does indicate that humans have some duty to consider them. He points out that human beings by virtue of their superior intelligence are 'capable of sympathising not solely with their offspring...but with all human and even with all sentient, beings.' The logic of his basic doctrine would indicate that the interests of sentient beings certainly cannot be ignored since they do have some capacity for pleasure and pain.

Later utilitarian thinkers, most notably Peter Singer, have certainly built on the logic of this aspect of Mill's thinking to argue that utilitarianism cannot ignore the interests of sentient animals for the obvious reason that they can experience pain and pleasure in some form.

If we argue that it is a logical extension of Mill's theory to include all sentient beings, then this will have clear implications for our treatment of environmental resources as well as levels of pollution. Destruction of natural habitats for example (e.g. rainforest areas) leads to loss of biodiversity and even the extinction of some animals. Pollution whether from acid rain or oil tankers has caused massive loss of animal life.

Another difference between Mill and Bentham concerns Mill's distinction between 'higher' and 'lower' pleasures. While Bentham argues that there are only differences in quantity between pleasures (i.e. is there more or less pleasure to be gained form pushpin or poetry), Mill argues that there are also differences in quality. It is a higher quality pleasure Mill might say for example to write poetry than to play pushpin. Higher pleasures are those of the mind, while lower or 'swine' pleasures are merely those of the body. This distinction can easily be applied to the modern consumer lifestyle and its detrimental impact on the environment in terms of waste and pollution. Our pursuit of physical comfort beyond what is purely necessary, would clearly come into the category of 'lower pleasures'. It is an unsustainable lifestyle in that it places massive demands upon natural resources and leads almost inevitably to pollution.

▶PETER SINGER

Peter Singer (1946-) is an Australian philosopher who firmly places his work in the tradition of utilitarianism. He is best known for his often controversial application of utilitarian principles to environmental issues, and in particular the treatment of animals.

Singer argues that attempts to build ethics on the "will of God" fail because of the problem raised centuries ago by Plato in the so-called "Eutyphro dilemma"[xvi]. Singer finds other forms of deontological ethics such as that of Kant (see next section) inadequate in part because of the problem raised where different absolute moral rules conflict[xvii].

Faced with these problems Singer reaches his utilitarian position 'by universalising self-interested decision making'[xviii]. He argues that all humans seek after their own interests, and animals also have interests which they seek after although they are in general less conscious of those interests e.g. the interest in their survival. Most people tend to put the pursuit of their interests above the pursuit of other peoples' interests and certainly above the interests of animals, but Singer argues that rationally there is no reason why one being's interests should take precedence over those of another being. As Singer puts in the context of a discussion on the distribution of wealth, 'From an ethical point of view, the fact that it is I who benefit say from a more equal distribution of income and you who lose by it, is irrelevant'[xix]. Ethics therefore involves taking the 'universal' and 'objective' point of view when making a decision thus taking into account all the interests that will be affected by a certain decision. Singer assures his readers that if this rational approach is taken 'an ethically good life is also a good life for the person leading it'[xx].

When taking the universal point of view therefore there can be no room for favouring one group of people above another on the grounds of race for example, but also no room for favouring one species above another. Singer summarises his argument for this as follows:

'The argument for extending the principle of equality beyond our own species is simple…it amounts to no more than a clear understanding of the nature of the principle of the equal consideration of interests…our concern for others ought not to depend on what they are like, or what abilities they possess…The capacity for suffering and enjoying things is a prerequisite for having interests at all, a condition that must be satisfied before we can speak of interests in any meaningful way. It would be nonsense to say that it was not in the interests of a stone to be kicked along a road by a schoolboy. A stone does not have interests because it cannot suffer. Nothing that we could possibly do to it could possibly make any difference to its welfare. A mouse on the other hand does have an interest in not being tormented, because mice will suffer if they are treated in this way'[xxi].

Most controversially Singer argues that some of the higher animals such as chimpanzees may have 'interests' that actually carry more weight than those humans with severe mental disability because such humans have no self-awareness and thus no fear of their own end. Chimps on the other hand show sign of self-consciousness and thus have a greater stake or interest in the preservation of their lives.

Singer is clear therefore that in reference to environmental issues we should be concerned with the 'interests of sentient creatures, present and future, human and non-human'[xxii]. He illustrates the implications of this position with reference to the issue of whether or not to dam a river;

> 'If the decision were to be made on the basis of human interest alone, we would balance the economic benefits of the dam for the citizens of the state against the loss for bushwalkers, scientists, and others, now and in the future, who value the preservation of the river in its natural state. We have already seen that because the calculation includes an indefinite number of future generations, the loss of the wild river is a much greater cost than we might at first imagine. Even so, once we broaden the basis of our decision beyond the interests of human beings, we have much more to set against the economic benefits of building the dam. Into the calculations must now go the interests of all the non-human animals who live in the area that will be flooded... Neither drowning or starvation are easy ways to die, and the suffering involved in these deaths should, as we have seen, be given no less weight than we would give to an equivalent amount of suffering experienced by human beings... utilitarians will take into account the loss that death inflicts on the animals—the loss of all their future existence, and the experiences that their future lives would have contained'[xxiii].

▶ POSSIBLE PROBLEMS WITH UTILITARIAN APPROACHES TO THE ENVIRONMENT

Broadly these come into two categories.

First, objections can be raised against the theory of utilitarianism as a whole. These include:

- Opponents of utilitarianism sometimes argue that when people think and speak about moral matters, they presuppose that absolute moral rules exist which have authority independently of whether following them creates pleasure or pain. Indeed humans discover these rules existing independently of them rather than creating those rules themselves. Those people may not be sure of where those absolute moral rules come from particularly in the absence of any belief in God, but nevertheless they believe that there are objective, absolute rules "set in stone". Utilitarians deny this, arguing that all rules are human creations initially designed to promote pleasure and reduce pain. In doing this, they ignore a fundamental human intuition about the nature of morality.

- Utilitarianism may also ignore the fundamental human belief that humans should never be used as "means to an end". Within a utilitarian view it may be possible to occasionally justify treating an individual unfairly if the majority benefits as a result. For example, giving a criminal an unfairly severe sentence in order to deter other criminals thereby benefiting wider society at the expense of that individual. Treating the criminal as a means to the end of benefiting society in this way violates the human conviction that each individual should be treated in accordance with what they deserve. Furthermore, expecting people to be involved in a system that does treat people as means to an end (e.g. the judge sentencing the criminal to an unfair sentence) is asking them to violate their own code of ethics.

- Other opponents argue that utilitarianism particularly in its "act-utilitarian" form is simply impractical as a guide to making decisions. When making a decision it is impossible to weigh up all the possible pains and pleasures that may result from an action. Life is inevitably unpredictable, so it is impossible to predict with certainty that a particular decision will lead to a particular amount of pleasure or pain.

Second, stemming from these broader criticisms come problems with utilitarianism in relation to environmental issues particularly:

- A utilitarian view of the environment has in the past often allowed people to simply exploit nature for short-term human benefit. This violates the absolute rights of respect which nature has. The source of these rights might be belief in nature as the creation of God, or belief in nature as in some other way sacred[xxiv].

- While it is increasingly accepted that we should meet the needs of present generations without compromising the ability of future generations to meet their needs, it is very difficult to make this sort of utilitarian calculation. The problem comes in actually defining the reasonable needs of the present, particularly since we cannot know for certain what the needs of the future will be. How far into the future should a utilitarian look? How far into the future can we look given the technical advances that are likely to be made which we as yet know nothing of?

- The danger exists that when making environmental decisions from a utilitarian perspective we treat certain groups as means to the end of the happiness of the majority. For example, because the majority's happiness is served by allowing them to drive cars in urban environments the health of children and other vulnerable groups is adversely affected by the resulting air pollution. The health of future generations is sacrificed in innumerable ways as the current generation seeks to maximise its pleasure.

The following case study indicates some of the problems that utilitarians might face when approaching environmental dilemmas:

> Case study on the Bakun hydroelectric dam in Sarawak, Malaysian Borneo:
>
> Faced with massive demands for electricity among its growing urban populace, coupled with those from rapid industrialisation, the Malaysian government has been left needing significantly more electricity supply. In response to this need the government intends to build a hydroelectric dam on one of its rivers. The dam will be a kilometre long and 200 m high stretching across the fast-flowing Balui river. After its proposed completion in 2002, the dam will flood 700 square km of rain forest and farmland displacing nine thousand indigenous people. Rare species of plant and animal would also be lost in the process, and in all probability the unique culture of the indigenous peoples would be lost. This would also be a huge loss to future generations. On the positive side it is estimated that the energy produced by the dam could supply up to 20 million homes with electricity. Furthermore, hydroelectric technology is a "cleaner" technology environmentally than nuclear or fossil-fuel power stations.

The utilitarian conundrum of what to do in this situation is intensified by some of the arguments put forward by those against the dam. They point for example to the energy that is currently wasted in Malaysian cities by the failure to conserve more energy. Installing low-energy light bulbs and insulating air-conditioned buildings would at the very least reduce the need for these sort of projects. Equally they point out that a stepped series of smaller dams up the river valley would flood far less land and ease boat travel. They also point to developing energy technologies such as solar power which in the future might render such massive projects unnecessary. Finally they argue that the money spent on the dam (estimated at $5.5 billion) could be better spent helping the Malaysian poor out of their poverty.

Proponents of the dam counter these assertions by arguing that the sheer scale of the electricity demands of the Malaysian populace necessitate this project. Nothing else will satisfy the demand. They point to the interests of the bulk of the Malaysian populace outweighing those of the indigenous minority.

Faced with these different arguments the utilitarian task is difficult, if not impossible.

▶KANTIAN PERSPECTIVES ON THE ENVIRONMENT

Kant (1724-1804) developed a very different approach to ethics compared to that of Bentham, Mill and Singer. His approach to ethical decision-making can be applied to environmental issues, but it is important to bear in mind that environmental issues were not as much of an issue in the eighteenth century as they are today. Therefore Kant has nothing to say directly on the sort of environmental problems preoccupying contemporary generations. However later philosophers have taken some of his basic ideas and applied then to modern environmental issues. It is also legitimate for you to find your own ways in which his thinking might be applied to these issues as long as you can demonstrate that your ideas are consistent with his thought.

▶SUMMARY OF KANT'S BASIC IDEAS[xxv]:

- Kant rejects all consequentialist accounts of ethics i.e. those that judge actions in references to their outcomes, and thereby produce hypothetical imperatives (i.e. "Do this if you want this outcome").

- Kant stresses that humans are distinguished from other life forms by their capacity to 'reason' about ethics. Their reason not their instinct, desire or emotion should guide their actions.

Reason produces 2 imperatives or rules in particular that should be followed 'categorically' (i.e. automatically, with no exceptions, and no reference to consequences). Kant's system is therefore rule-based; a 'deontological' system.

These categorical imperatives are:

A] 'Act only on that maxim whereby you can at the same time will that it should become universal law' (The Formula of Universal Law).

B] 'Act so as to treat humanity never only as a means but always also as an end' (The Formula of the End in itself).

To always obey reason and follow the Categorical imperative is to demonstrate a 'good will' by acting in accord with 'duty'.

Kant's thinking has been applied by later philosophers to environmental issues in the following ways:

- R.Hepburn in his book Wonder and Other Essays[xxvi] builds on Kant's Formula of the End in itself, arguing that it can legitimately be made to relate to the proper human response to the natural environment. This proper response according to Hepburn is one of 'wonder'. This attitude of wonder is non-utilitarian and non-exploitative i.e. it is not looking at the natural environment in terms of how it can be exploited for the needs of human beings. It is characterised by the following attitudes towards the natural world; respect, compassion, gentleness and humility.

Hepburn sees some roots for this attitude in Kant's general thinking and his Formula of the End in itself in particular. He alerts us to Kant's famous statement:

'Two things fill the mind with even new and increasing admiration and awe, the oftener and more steadily we reflect on them: the starry heavens above and the moral law within.'

Kant clearly had some sense of what Hepburn would label 'wonder' in relation to the natural environment and would presumably have been very concerned about actions that threaten it.

Furthermore Kant's Formula of the End in Itself in its emphasis on respect for people as Ends can legitimately be applied to a wider range of things than just rational beings. Of course Hepburn accepts that Kant only applied it to rational, human beings, but he observes how the underlying logic of the imperative seems to require a broader application. If I treat something as a means to an end of mine, and only as a means, I treat it as having no value that is independent of how it meets my needs and desires. To treat something as an End therefore is to imply that it has a value independently of me. This would then place restrictions on how it might be treated.

To Hepburn this attitude of respect that Kant only explicitly relates to human, reasoning agents implicitly can be used to rule out 'acts of vandalism and thoughtless manipulation' in relation to the natural world. Furthermore Hepburn says 'the nearer the [natural] object comes to having the life, sentience, and rational powers proper to moral personhood, the more the element of respect in wonder takes on the Kantian quality'. Although Hepburn does not give any examples, we might think that certain higher animals such as apes and chimpanzees begin to come into this category.

Overall then Hepburn is arguing three things:

1] Kant had an admiration and awe for the natural world which would have made him uneasy with simply giving it an instrumental value in relation to human needs.

2] The "spirit" behind the Formula of the End in Itself (i.e. not to treat things merely as means to your end) permits a broader application to many parts of the natural world than Kant explicitly gives it.

3] Therefore, the exploitation for personal ends of natural resources and the resultant pollution, should be stopped.

- Paul Taylor in his book *Respect for Nature: A theory of environmental Ethics*[xxvii] consciously builds on Kant's ethical system, and in particular the second formulation of the Categorical imperative, to argue for a non-exploitative respect and care for the natural world.

His theory is based on two closely related ideas whose relation to Kantian ideas should be quite obvious:

The concept of inherent worth:

Taylor states: 'To have the attitude of respect for nature is to regard the wild plants and animals of the Earth's ecosystems as possessing inherent worth. That such creatures have inherent worth may be considered the fundamental value presupposition of the attitude of respect'. By inherent worth Taylor means that nature does not just have value as a means to the fulfilment of human ends (e.g. providing food for humans to eat). Rather it also has value simply in and of itself, whether or not it provides for humans.

For something to have inherent worth it is necessary that it has a 'good of its own':

Taylor explains; 'To say that an entity has a good of its own is simply to say that, without reference to any other entity, it can be benefited or harmed...We can think of the good of an individual non-human organism as consisting in the full development of its biological powers. Its good is realised to the extent that it is strong and healthy. It possesses whatever capacities it needs for successfully coping with its environment and so preserving its existence throughout the various stages of the normal lifecycle of its species.'

These two related ideas lead Taylor to a conclusion that deliberately echoes Kant:

'The assertion that an entity has inherent worth is here to be understood as entailing two moral judgements:

1] that the entity is deserving of moral concern and consideration, or in other words that it is a moral subject, and

2] that all moral agents have a prima facie[xxviii] duty to promote or preserve the entity's good as an end in itself and for the sake of the entity whose good it is'.

Basically then Taylor has extended Kant's idea of the respect due to humans as rational agents with their own Ends to every living organism, sentient or non-sentient. The organism may not be conscious of its own interests in the way in which humans (and higher animals) are, but nevertheless it has those interests according to Taylor. As long as it can be said to have those interests it must not be exploited and manipulated to serve human interests. Rather it must be treated as an End in itself.

- Several philosophers concerned with animal welfare have pointed out how recent discoveries concerning the rational and reflective capacities of certain higher animals (chimpanzees and dolphins would be the most obvious examples) simply would not have been available to Kant. If they had been there might well be reason to suppose that Kant would have extended the range of sentient beings who should be treated as Ends to include them.

This blurring of the distinction between humans and animals has also occurred as a result of our increasing genetic knowledge. For example, we now know that chimps and humans share 98% of the same DNA (even tree bark shares 50% of its genetic material with humans!).

This blurring, some philosophers argue, is sufficient to extend the second categorical imperative to cover the interests of all sentient beings, some of which may also be rational beings in a very limited way (no more limited though than very severely mentally disabled humans).

▶ POSSIBLE PROBLEMS WITH KANTIAN APPROACHES TO THE ENVIRONMENT

- Some have questioned how far the work of Hepburn and Taylor can be said to be a genuine development of Kant's actual philosophy. Kant clearly intends that the Categorical Imperative should be applied to humans in their relations with other humans. At no point does he make reference to how either form of the Categorical Imperative might be applied to non-human animals or the natural world in general.

- Kant's view expressed in the 'Formula of the End in Itself' that humans, because they are free, rational beings should be treated as "ends" not "means". This idea is closely linked to the rest of his philosophy, and in particular his view of human nature. He argues that while at one level, the level of appearances (what Kant calls the 'phenomenal' level), humans seem to lack any freedom, governed as they are by instincts and other physical factors, at another level beyond that of experience (the 'noumenal' level), humans actually are free. Hence their freedom should be respected by treating them as ends not means. It is the reality of the noumenal dimension which exists beyond experience and therefore beyond scientific detection, that leads to his view that humans should be treated as ends not means. However this idea of the noumenal dimension has been attacked by many philosophers as an idea which while attractive, is impossible to verify by any method; it is little more than a "leap of faith", and therefore an inadequate base for his ethical system.
- Other aspects of Kant's moral philosophy can also be questioned[xxix]. In particular there is no room in Kant's approach to ethics for virtues such as generosity, benevolence, compassion, or sympathy. The morally correct action according to Kant is simply one that follows the demands of reason expressed in the Categorical Imperative. Feelings of benevolence, compassion etc. should be avoided since they will only get in the way of the correct application of the Categorical Imperative. However, to most people such feelings are morally good and necessary to successful human relationships. Kant has missed an important element of human moral behaviour.

▶RELIGIOUS PERSPECTIVES ON ENVIRONMENTAL ISSUES

All religions have views on the environment which are clearly of significance for the adherents of these faiths. However these views are also of wider significance since they have shaped society's views in the past, and to some degree today, on the environment, whether the society acknowledges that debt or not. So for example, while many contemporary Westerners no longer believe in a God who created the earth, they may still view the earth as in some ways sacred and to be protected. We will briefly discuss a Christian response, which overlaps with many aspects of a Jewish response, and then a Buddhist response. These two have been chosen because Christianity is a theistic faith, whereas Buddhism does not believe in any transcendent, omnipotent and creative God responsible for the universe. Nevertheless both have strong views on environmental issues.

WHAT ARE SOME OF THE RELIGIOUS PERSPECTIVES?

▶ ARE JEWISH AND CHRISTIAN VIEWS TO BLAME FOR MUCH OF CURRENT EXPLOITATION AND ABUSE OF THE ENVIRONMENT?

Two allegations are made against Christianity by non-Christian philosophers such as Peter Singer:

- Whereas before Judaeo-Christian thought, nature was full of spirits (animism) or identical with God (pantheism), Judaeo-Christian thought insisted that the natural world was devoid of such presences. Nature was the inanimate creation of God. This paved the way for fearless exploitation of nature e.g. the tree spirit would not mind if people chopped down a tree because there was no such spirit.

- Genesis, which sets the scene for all subsequent Jewish and Christian thought on nature, sets humans up as the peerless masters of nature who are to use it for their own ends. This paves the way for exploitation.

While it is true that some Christians have used their faith as a justification for environmental exploitation, in many ways this critical analysis is aimed at a false caricature of the Jewish and Christian views of the environment. These views if properly understood demonstrate the following features that arguably lead away from an exploitative attitude to nature, towards a caring, responsible and respectful attitude. In what follows the Christian views mentioned stem largely from Biblical material. A fuller examination of the Christian position would involve discussion of Natural Law perspectives and that of key figures through Christian tradition.

The relevant Biblical material is set out under three categories to highlight the breadth of material that can be applied to environmental issues. The categories follow the course of God's involvement with the human race according to Christian belief.

▶ THE EARTH AS THE CREATION OF GOD

Christian attitudes to the environment are based on the belief that the earth, indeed the whole universe, was designed and created by God as described in the Bible. This is developed in the following ways:

1] God, as creator of the earth (Genesis 1-2), is the rightful owner of the world. He declares that his creation is 'very good' (Genesis 1:31). This is an intrinsic or inherent good, not an extrinsic good because it serves the needs of humans. While God is therefore the rightful owner and ruler of the world, He has conferred the right and responsibility to rule upon humans. Humans must therefore take care to preserve the world in the beauty and order that led God to declare it 'very good'. Humans do not have the authority to do what they like with the creation, because they are only ruling (See Psalm 8:6) on behalf of the Creator God. Humans are "Stewards" of the world on God's behalf.

> Psalm 24:1-2 'The earth is the Lord's, and everything in it, the world and all that live in it; for he founded it in the seas and established it upon the waters'

2] Humans are made in the image of God (Genesis 1:27). This basically means that humans are made in such a way that they "stand in" for God in the world. They are to rule and look after the world in a way consistent with their Creator. In doing this they are to reflect, like a mirror image, the concerns and nature of God. So how does God treat nature? The following sort of passages make it clear:

> 'He (i.e. God) makes springs pour water into the ravines:
> it flows between the mountains.
> They give water to all the beasts of the field:
> the wild donkeys quench their thirst.
> The birds of the air nest by the waters;
> they sing among the branches.
> He waters the mountains from his upper chambers;
> the earth is satisfied by the fruit of his work.
> He makes grass grow for the cattle...'(Psalm 104)

This passage along with many other reveals the sort of God upon whose behalf humans are called to rule the earth. Human rule must reflect God's rule, and that is one of care rather than exploitation.

3] Humans are instructed by God in Genesis to

'Be fruitful and increase in number; fill the earth and subdue it. Rule over the fish of the sea and the birds of the air and over every living creature that moves on the ground'(Genesis 1:28)

Later their task is described as follows

'The Lord God took the man and put him in the Garden of Eden to work it and take care of it'(Genesis 2:15)

Some have seen the 'subdue' and 'rule' as having harsh connotations that humans may exploit for their own ends. However, in the context of Genesis and the rest of the Old Testament, this interpretation is wrong. Furthermore the fact that Adam and Eve were to be vegetarians in the Garden of Eden indicates that the emphasis was far more on care than on any exploitation.

4] Many passages in the Old Testament make it clear that the natural environment should point to, and reflect the goodness and glory of God. Humans as stewards on God's behalf of that creation must therefore do all they can to ensure that the natural environment continues to reflect the glory of God. One such passage is Psalm 19 which starts,

> 'The heavens (i.e.skies) declare the glory of God;
> the skies proclaim the work of his hands.
> Day after day they pour forth speech; night after night
> they display knowledge.
> There is no speech or language
> where their voice is not heard.
> Their voice goes out into all the earth, their words
> to the ends of the world' (Psalm 19:1-4).

Pollution, destruction of natural habitats for industrial farming, skin cancers from ozone depletion...do not 'declare the glory of God'.

▷ Israel (i.e. what would become of the Jewish nation)—a pattern for all nations to follow in regard to the environment

1] The land does not belong ultimately to the Israelites therefore they cannot simply do what they want with it. Just like Adam and Eve were, they are stewards of God's possession, and must work to fulfill His plans for the earth.

> 'The Land must not be sold permanently, because the land is mine and you are but aliens and tenants'(Leviticus25:23)

2] God's plans for the earth include a concern for the welfare of non-human animals and plants, trees etc (i.e. the whole ecosystem), as well as the welfare of humans who must all be provided for from the produce of the land. Several verses from the Old Testament illustrate God's concern for the natural environment and animals. For example:

> 'In the seventh year the land is to have a Sabbath of rest, a Sabbath to the Lord. Do not sow your fields or prune your vineyards or harvest the grapes of your untended vines' (Leviticus25:4-6)

> 'Six days do your work, but on the seventh day do not work, so that your ox and your donkey may rest and the slave born in your household, and the alien as well, may be refreshed'(Exodus23:12)

Exploitation of natural environments therefore was outlawed for two reasons: it would damage the natural habitat itself, and threaten the animals living within those habitats. God is thought of as concerned with both.

▶ THE EXAMPLE OF JESUS AND THE EARLY CHURCH IN RELATION TO THE NATURAL ENVIRONMENT:

1] Jesus repeatedly criticises greed for more wealth and possessions. For example,

> 'No-one can serve two masters. Either he will hate the one and love the other, or he will be devoted to one and despise the other. You cannot serve both God and money '(Matthew 6:24)

Instead, wealth should be given away whenever possible,

> 'Sell your possessions and give to the poor. Provide purses for yourselves that will not wear out, a treasure in heaven that will not be exhausted, where no thief comes near and no moth destroys. For where your treasure is, there your heart will be also' (Luke12:33-34)

Christians today often apply this emphasis on the dangers of greed to the modern consumer lifestyle which relies heavily on the continued exploitation and overuse of the natural environment. Such a lifestyle, they argue, is inconsistent with the teaching of Jesus.

2] Jesus' teaching reveals a deep interest in the natural world and a belief in the love of God for the whole of the non-human creation. For example,

> 'Do not worry... Look at the birds of the air; they do not sow or reap or store away in barns, and yet your heavenly Father feeds them... And why do you worry about clothes? See how the lilies of the field grow. They do not labour or spin. Yet I tell you that not even Solomon dressed in all his splendour was dressed like one of these. If that is how God clothes the grass of the field...will he not much more clothe you...' (Matt 6:25-30)

3] The early church cannot have inflicted much damage on the environment as a result of their levels of consumption. They lived quite frugally sharing their houses and possessions among one another according to the need of each member of the community, as well as needy outsiders (See Acts 2:44). They certainly modelled a very different lifestyle from that of many modern Westerners whose levels of consumption do directly affect the environment for the worse.

▶BUDDHIST ATTITUDES TO THE ENVIRONMENT:

In the Buddha's first sermon given to the five ascetics with whom he had previously trained, He set out the Four Noble Truths that embodied the heart of his teaching.

A summary of the Four Noble Truths:
1] Dukkha: The reality of life is suffering.
2] Tanha: Greed or desire which is the cause of human suffering.
3] Nirodha: There can be an end to suffering if the following step is taken;
4] Magga: The middle-way between luxury and poverty should be followed.

Magga or the middle-way is described elsewhere within the Buddha's teaching as an eight-fold path with eight particular characteristics, but even the most basic idea of middle way between excessive luxury and extreme poverty reveals an important Buddhist insight into environmental issues. Many of the contemporary problems faced by the environment stem from a demand for goods that are not necessary for a healthy, balanced life, but rather stem from a greedy desire for ever-higher standards of luxury. The Second Noble Truth Buddhists argue also reveals that it is a mistake to assume that owning more and more possessions at the cost of the environment will bring lasting happiness anyway. Rather ownership of these goods will simply lead to a desire for more possessions and so on. The example of the Buddha's own life according to Buddhists illustrates powerfully how a very luxurious life such as that led by the Buddha in his childhood fails to tackle the reality of human suffering.

Within the eight-fold path great attention is paid to right action i.e. those actions which help one along the path to enlightenment. Such actions should obey the following rules in particular:

The Five Precepts:
Each of the Five Precepts has a positive and negative aspect:
- I undertake to abstain from taking life //
  By deeds of loving kindness I purify my body.
- I undertake to abstain from taking what is not freely given //
  With open-handed generosity I purify my body.
- I undertake to abstain from the misuse of the senses //
  With stillness, simplicity and contentment I purify my body.
- I undertake to abstain from wrong speech //
  With truthful communication I purify my speech.
- I undertake to abstain from taking drugs and alcohol which cloud the mind //
  With mindfulness, clear and radiant, I purify my mind.

Several of these precepts have considerable implications for environmental issues according to Buddhists. Three examples will illustrate:

First, many Buddhists link the First Precept with the issue of ahimsa, meaning harmlessness, to argue for vegetarian lifestyles. The First Precept applies to all sentient beings, and hence plants are excluded.

Any intentional taking or that will occur through negligence therefore is wrong. The killing of animals for food therefore is considered wrong unless human survival depends on it. Indeed, Buddhist monks have been known to apply the First Precept so strictly that they use a water strainer when drinking to check that there are no living creatures in their water, and to avoid travel during the rainy season when creatures may be washed onto the ground in the water and killed by means of transport. Some Buddhist monks frowned on the practice of ploughing since creatures may be killed in the process. Some Buddhists are vegan i.e. they abstain from any products taken from animals, even milk, cheese etc.

Given this commitment to animal welfare, Buddhists will be very concerned about environmental problems such as pollution, which can threaten whole animal populations e.g. oil spills from tankers which kill off bird species, and deforestation which destroys the natural habitat of many animals.

Second, environmental problems also lead to enormous suffering even destruction of life among humans in direct violation therefore of the First Precept. For example, soil erosion in the Developing world caused particularly by deforestation and over-use of the land through poverty, leads to inadequate soil for growth of crops, and eventually starvation of humans and also their livestock.

Third, many Buddhists link the Second Precept to environmental issues through consideration of future generations of humans. They argue that the earth is not a possession of humans living today which they can treat in any way they please. It has not been 'freely given' to this generation to do what it likes with. By exploiting it therefore, humans are in effect stealing from future generations who will not have a chance to enjoy the resources which they have as much right to as people living today. Contemporary generations are not acting with 'open-handed generosity' when they destroy living species through their actions, or deplete the ozone layer thereby threatening the welfare of many in the future.

Buddhists also often link other aspects of their key beliefs to environmental issues. For example, the belief in karma. Buddhists not only believe in individual karma which leads to consequences in that individual's life, but also in collective karma of the whole human race. Just as an individual's bad actions can lead to negative consequences for him or her, so they "feed into" a bad collective karma which is believed to lead to the environmental problems which we are seeing today. Buddhists express this through the belief in paticcasamupadda, or the Principle of conditionality.

Paticcasamupadda teaches that
- everything comes into being and is maintained by a complex web of conditions
- everything is part of the network of conditions maintaining something else
- nothing exists completely independent of anything else
- everything ceases when the conditions that maintain it cease
- the whole of existence is a ceaseless process of flux and change
- conditionality applies on all levels of existence from the physical environment to the human mind[xxx].

▶POSSIBLE PROBLEMS WITH RELIGIOUS APPROACHES TO THE ENVIRONMENT:

- Some critics point to the gap that has existed between theory and practice in religious responses to the environment through history. For example, while Buddhism may theoretically foster good attitudes towards the environment, countries with majority Buddhist populations today are very far from being role-models for environmental good practice. However, Buddhists will often respond that the lack of environmental good practice results from the pressures of living within a global economy that as a whole does not respect the rights and needs of the environment. They will point out recent Buddhist initiatives designed to model a sustainable approach to the environment[xxxi].

- In order to really grasp the significance of religious approaches to the environment, it is necessary to share the underlying religious convictions. It is impossible to really understand for example the Christian idea of human stewardship of nature without accepting the existence of a Creator God who made humans for a particular purpose. Religious views of the environment therefore could never become a blueprint for the behaviour of all people since people have different views on religious matters. Some Christians, and Buddhists may respond at this point by arguing that the views of their religion on the environment make sense even to those who do not buy into the rest of that religion. The idea of stewardship for example can be appreciated by those who do not accept every aspect of Christianity, but do accept that the natural world is in some way sacred and to be protected.

- There are often significant differences in the interpretation of religious texts in relation to environmental issues. For example, some have seen some of the texts from Genesis examined earlier as fostering an exploitative attitude towards nature, while other have seen them as encouraging sensible, sustainable use of natural resources. Some critics argue therefore that it is impossible to build an ethical system on such an ambiguous basis. However adherents of different faiths will often reply that while there have always been different interpretations of religious texts, this does not automatically mean that no interpretation is more correct than any other. For example, it may be true that exploitative interpretations of Genesis were actually a misreading of the text which in the light of increasing knowledge and skill of interpretation can be put right.

WORKSHEET

1] Outline the principle causes and consequences of:
   a) Global Warming
   b) Reduction in natural habitats
   c) Depletion of the Ozone Layer

2] What objections exist to taking drastic steps to reduce the production of Greenhouse Gases?

3] Identify the basic similarities and differences between "act" and "rule" utilitarianism.

4] Identify the key similarities and differences between Bentham's version of utilitarianism, and that of Mill.

5] Why does Singer argue that the interests of all sentient organisms should be taken into account when making environmental decisions?

6] Identify the key strengths and weaknesses in your view of utlitarianism as set out by:
a) Bentham   b) Mill   c) Singer

7] (i) How might a]Hepburn and b]Taylor, be said to build on the ethical philosophy of Kant?
   (ii) In your opinion are they really building on Kant's ideas or actually manipulating them for their own ends?

8] Outline the Christian view on the role humans are meant to play in relation to the natural world.

9] How might the example of Jesus and the early church affect Christian responses to the environment?

10] In what ways can the Five Precepts of Buddhism be applied to environmental issues?

11] Does Buddhism in your opinion provide a useful set of perspectives and guidelines on treating the natural world properly?

ANSWERING EXAM QUESTIONS

In questions on religious and/or philosophical approaches to environmental issues, it is important to strike a balance between writing too much and too little on the actual environmental issues. It is necessary to show the examiner that, for example, in a question dealing with global warming you know the basic causes and consequences of the rise in global temperature, but not necessarily to go into great scientific detail on the subject. Your knowledge of the science should always be linked to answering the actual question set.

Candidates are often stronger on philosophical responses to environmental issues than religious responses. It is important to answer all components of a question to an equal standard.

Sample question

'Utilitarianism provides a better guide to deciding on contemporary environmental problems than religion'. Explain and assess this claim.

Answer plan

[It is legitimate given time pressures, to move straight into the main body of your answer. If you have time to set out a brief introduction, simply inform the examiner of the structure of the answer you are about to give]

Set out how a utilitarian might approach environmental issues. Choose either Bentham, Mill or Singer. If time you may discuss more than one of these. Note if dealing with Singer be careful to explain why he can be described as a utilitarian. Choose, depending on time, one or two particular environmental problems e.g. Ozone depletion or loss of natural habitats.

Emphasise the strengths of the utilitarian view e.g. it is a flexible system built on the reasonable assumption that pleasure/happiness is a good thing.

Set out the key components of a religious approach to the environment. It is probably better to deal with one religious tradition in some detail although the question would allow a more general discussion that referred in specific detail to several religious traditions.

Highlight some alleged weaknesses of this religious approach.

Assess the relative strength of the argument "quoted" in the question, and explained so far by your answer:

If you are largely in agreement with the argument, explain why it convinces you. If you find yourself in danger of repeating arguments given earlier, explain why you do not agree with the sort of counter-arguments that might be put against it.

If you disagree with it, explain why, making sure you criticise the strengths you outlined earlier.

Come to a conclusion, making sure that your conclusion follows from the rest of your argument.

FURTHER READING

On philosophical approaches to ethics generally:

Ethics Piers Benn (UCL Press 1999) ISBN 1-85728-453-4
Readability: **** Content: ####
Includes good explanations of utilitarian and Kantian thought.

Ethics ed. Peter Singer (OUP 2000)   ISBN 0-19-289245-2
Readability: ** Content: ###
contains passages from Mill, Bentham and Kant

Ethics Mel Thompson ISBN 0-340-61101-4
Readability: *** Content: ###
Basic introduction to moral philosophy.

A Short History of Ethics A.Macintyre ISBN 0-415-040272
Readability:* Content: ###
More advanced look at major themes in moral philosophy including utlitarianism and Kant.

Practical Ethics 2nd ed. Peter Singer CUP 0-521-43971-X
Readability: *** Content: ##
A good defence of Singer's views in general with a chapter on the environment.

How are we to live? Peter Singer (OUP 1997)
Readability: **** Content: ##
A popular explanation of Singer's ideas.

Utilitarianism and its Critics ed. J.Glover (Macmillan 1990)
ISBN 0-02-344134-8
Readability:* Content:##
More difficult, but worthwhile selection of critical issues.

Issues facing Christians today John Stott
(London, Marshall Pickering 1990 Note: since reprinted)
Readability: **** Content: ###
Thorough treatment of Christian approaches to ethical issues including the environment.

An Introduction to Buddhist Ethics P.Harvey (CUP 2000)
ISBN 0521 55640 6
Readability: * Content: ###
Quite advanced and very thorough exploration of Buddhist ethics, including a chapter on the environment.

On the state of the environment:

State of the World written annually by World Watch Institute and published by London, Earthscan
Readability: ** Content: ###
A thorough guide to the latest environmental developments.

Poverty and the Planet Ben Jackson (Harmondsworth, Penguin 1994)
Readability: *** Content:###
An excellent exploration of political and economic background to environmental problems.

Global Warming: The Complete Briefing John Houghton (Oxford, Lion 1994).
Readability: ** Content:##
Thorough treatment of Global Warming.

The Sceptical Environmentalist: Measuring the real state of the world Bjorn Lomborg (CUP 2001)
Readability: * Content: ###
A sceptical look at many environmental "problems" and their proposed solutions, arguing that there are far more urgent issues facing the world than those chosen by the environmental lobby.
The *New Internationalist* magazine available from most good newsagents often contains useful material. See no. 78 in particular (New Internationalist Publications 1996).

Works on environmental ethics:

Environmental Ethics J.Walker (Hodder&Stoughton 2000)
ISBN 0 340 75770 1
Readability: **** Content: ###
A good introduction aimed at AS/A2 Level students

Environmental Ethics: An introduction with readings
ed. John Benson (Routledge 2000) ISBN 0 415 21236 7
Readability: ** Content: ###
More advanced, wide-ranging look at modern philosophical approaches to environmental issues.

Green Christianity Tim Cooper (London, Spire 1990)
Readability: *** Content: ###
A good guide to modern Christian thinking on the environment.

God of the Poor Dewi Hughes and Matthew Bennett (OM Publishing 1999) ISBN 1-8078-297-0
Readability: *** Content: ##
A useful chapter on Christian responses to environmental issues.

Pollution and the Death of Man F.Schaeffer (Wheaton, Illinois, Crossway 1992)
Readability: * Content: ##
An important work in the development of Christian responses to the environment.

Buddhism and Ecology ed. M.Batchelor and K.Brown (London and New York, Cassell 1992) Sponsored by the World Wide Fund for Nature
Readability and content vary according to contributor, but generally useful.

KEY	Readability	* manageable;	** good;
		*** very good;	**** excellent.
	Content	# adequate;	## good;
		### very good;	#### excellent.

FOOTNOTES

i   The Guardian July 14 2001
ii   See website http://www.ipcc.ch
iii The Guardian August 23 2000. For more details see J.Houghton Global Warming: The Complete Briefing (Oxford, Lion 1994).
iv See for example Bjorn Lomborg The Sceptical Environmentalist: Measuring the real state of the world (CUP 2001)
v   Desertification, as the name implies, refers to the transition of previously fertile land into desert. The zone of Africa immediately south of the Sahara desert (often referred to as Sub-Saharan Africa) is particularly prone to this effect.
vi P. Singer How are we to live? OUP 1997 p.53.
vii Jackson, B., Poverty and the Planet (Hardmondsworth, Penguin 1994) p.90.
viii See Dewi Hughes and Matthew Bennett God of the Poor OM Publishing 1998 ch.12
ix F. Pearce quoted in Walker, J Environmental Ethics (Hodder & Stoughton 2000) p.34.
x   P. Singer How are we to live? OUP 1997 p.51
xi P. Singer for example identifies his view with preference utilitarianism which he describes as follows, '[we should] judge actions not by their tendency to maximise pleasure or minimise pain, but with the extent to which they accord with the preferences of any beings affected by the action or its consequences' (from P. Singer Practical Ethics CUP 1999 p.94).
xii J. Bentham Introduction to the Principles of Morals and Legislation (Hafner: New York, 1948) reprinted in Peter Singer ed. Ethics (Penguin 2000).
xiii Bentham radically wondered for example whether 'the day may come when the rest of animal creation may acquire those rights which never could have been withholden from them but by the hand of tyranny. The French have already discovered that the blackness of the skin is no reason why a human being should be abandoned without redress to the caprice of a tormentor. It may one day come to be recognised that the number of legs, the villosity of the skin, or the termination of the *os sacrum* are

reasons equally insufficient for abandoning a sensitive being to the same fate...The question is not, Can they reason? Nor Can they talk? But, Can they suffer?' (J.Bentham *Introduction to the Principles of Morals and Legislation* ch.18, sec.1,n.)

[xiv] J.S.Mill *On Liberty and other essays* OUP (recently reprinted)

[xv] See John Benson *Environmental Ethics. An introduction with readings* Routledge 2000 which contains a reprint of Mill's essay.

[xvi] The Eutyphro dilemma basically asks whether what God declares morally good is morally good because God labels it good, or whether it is morally good independently of God and God simply "informs humans of this fact. If one takes the latter alternative one is left with the fact that God actually becomes ultimately irrelevant to ethics since he is not the one who decides on right and wrong. However if one takes the former, Singer argues that one is left with the uncomfortable question of how we actually know whether what God labels as good is actually good. Maybe God is an evil being who labels evil things as good? Unless we have some standard of morality independent of God, how can we decide on the moral status of God?

[xvii] See Peter Singer *Practical Ethics* CUP 1999 pp.2–3.

[xviii] Op.Cit.p.14

[xix] Op.Cit.p.12

[xx] P. Singer *How are we to live?* OUP 1997 p.24

[xxi] Peter Singer *Practical Ethics* CUP 1999 p.63

[xxii] Peter Singer *Practical Ethics* CUP 1999 p.284

[xxiii] Op.Cit.pp.274–275

[xxiv] The Dalai Lama for example while not believing in any creator God maintains, 'The Earth, our Mother, is telling us to behave. All around, signs of nature's limitations abound...By protecting the natural environment...we show respect for Earth's human descendants...as well as for the natural right to life of all earth's living things'. Quoted in Joe Walker *Environmental Ethics* Hodder and Stoughton 2000

[xxv] For an introduction to Kant's thought see *Ethics* by Piers Benn UCVL Press 2000 For a more detailed look at his ethical thought see I.Kant *A Groundwork of the Metaphysics of Morals* (ed.Mary Gregor) CUP 2000

[xxvi] See John Benson *Environmental Ethics. An introduction with readings* Routledge 2000 p.203ff.
[xxvii] See John Benson *Environmental Ethics. An introduction with readings* Routledge 2000 p.215ff.
[xxviii] A prima facie duty is one that ought to be carried out unless there is, in the particular circumstances, another moral duty of over-riding importance.
[xxix] For a good discussion see A.MacIntyre *A Short History of Ethics* Routledge 1995 ch.9
[xxx] The Clear Vision Trust, Manchester 2000.
[xxxi] See material produced by The Clear Vision Trust, Manchester. Website: http://www.theredirectory.org.uk/orgs/cvt.html